Ninja CREAMi Cookbook
with Pictures

500 Days Tasty Ice Creams, Ice Cream Mix-Ins, Shakes, Sorbets, and Smoothies Recipes

for Beginners and Advanced Users

Tricia Howard

Introduction

What is Ninja CREAMi?

Ninja CREAMi is an efficient ice cream maker launched by Ninja Foodi. It can be used to prepare ice creams, smoothies, sorbets, and milkshakes in minimal time. The preparation process is very easy as you have to prepare the base, freeze the products overnight, and process the ingredients. The Ninja CREAMi uses state of the art CREAMify and dual drive motor technology, which easily converts everything into a smoothie form easily.

Main Functions of Ninja CREAMi

These functions include the following:

1. Ice Cream

This program is thoroughly designed for traditionally indulgent foods. It is best for transforming dairy and dairy alternative products into creamy, scoopable, and thick ice creams.

2. Lite Ice Cream

This program is extensively designed for health-conscious people to effectively preparing low-sugar, low fat or even sugar alternative ice creams.

3. Gelato

This program is basically designed for custard bases, specifically for ice creams (Italian-style). It is best suitable when your recipe surrounds an amazing and decadent dessert. This function is not available on all variants of the Ninja CREAMi.

4. Sorbet

This program is extensively designed for making fruit abundant recipes with high water and sugar into amazing creamy delights.

5. Milkshake

This program is designed to prepare thick and quick milkshakes. You can easily combine your favorite ice cream, mix-ins and milk and then press milkshake to get it ready for you in minimal time.

6. Smoothie Bowl

This program is specifically designed for recipes that involve both frozen or fresh fruits and even fresh or frozen veggies along with juice, dairy alternatives or dairy products. This function is not available on all variants of the Ninja CREAMi.

7. Mix-In

This function is specifically designed to fold in the pieces of nuts, frozen fruits, candies, cereal or cookies to customize a store-purchased treat or just-processed base thoroughly. This function is most suitable when used in the middle of the CREAMi Pint. Once the pint is processed, put a 1.5-inch hole using a spoon in the pint reaching down to the bottom, pour broken or chopped mix-ins through the hole and press the Mix-In function again.

8. Re-Spin

This program is extensively designed to thoroughly ensure a smooth and refined texture after efficiently running either of the preset programs. This function is optimally used when the base temperature is below -7° F, and the recipe texture is predominantly crumbly instead of creamy.

Tips

• Never use the Re-Spin program before using the Mix-In preset function.
• To thoroughly stop any preset program, press the illuminated program button.

Buttons & User Guide of Ninja CREAMi

The majority of the button and user guides have already been discussed in the portion above. Some of the relevant and essential button guides of the Ninja CREAMi is as follows:

Install Light

This light will glow when the Ninja CREAMi is not completely assembled. In case the light continues blinking, ensure that the bowl is placed correctly. If it glows constantly, check if the paddle is properly installed.

Progress Bar

The Progress Bar effectively displays the overall progress of the One-Touch Programs of the Ninja CREAMi. All of the four Progress Bar LEDs will thoroughly flash twice and subsequently turn off when once the program is complete.

One-Touch Programs

These preset programs last for 1-2 minutes are devised to whip up amazing creations in very minimal time. However, the programs might vary in speed and length depending upon the ideal settings to get perfect results for every specific recipe.

How to Clean & Maintain Ninja CREAMi?

Cleaning

We recommend you remove the CREAMizer Paddle from the Outer Bowl Lid. The outer bowl lid can be removed after thorough rinsing it and then subsequently pressing the paddle latch.

Hand Washing

As a general rule, always wash the lid, paddle and containers in warm soapy water. Use a dishwashing tool with a through handle for effective cleansing of the paddle. It would be best if you effectively rinsed and then thoroughly air-dry all the components.

Dish Washing

Lids, containers, and paddles are known to be dishwasher safe (only top rack). We recommend thoroughly separating the pint, lids, paddle, and outer bowl before putting them into the dishwasher. A dishwasher is an effective approach to remove ingredients that might stick to these components.

Maintenance

Outer Bowl Lid

We recommend you conveniently remove the paddle prior to cleaning the outer bowl lid, as there is a huge possibility of the leftover ingredients being stuck under the paddle.

Afterwards, thoroughly run warm water throughout the paddle, the drain holes, and the release lever on either of the sides. For fully draining the lid out, we recommend you to position the lid in such a manner that the lid is facing downwards. Moreover, efficiently take out the grey rubber lip seal that is thoroughly wrapped around the center of the outer bowl lid. Afterwards, thoroughly hand wash the seal and lid with warm soapy water, or you can even put it in the dishwasher.

Motor Base

First of all, unplug the motor base before cleaning to avoid any mishap. Use a damp cloth to clean the motor base effectively. We recommend you avoid using any pads, abrasive cloths, or brushes to clean the motor base effectively. We also recommend you use a damp cloth for effectively cleaning the swindle beneath the control panel after every use. We also recommend you thoroughly raise the platform for cleaning in case there is any trapped liquid between the motor base and the platform. Thoroughly put the outer bowl on the motor base with the handle positioned straight beneath the control panel and twist it towards the right to raise the platform effectively. Afterwards, use a damp cloth to thoroughly clean the portion between the raised platform and the motor base.

Vanilla Milkshake

Preparation Time: 10 minutes
Servings: 2

Ingredients:

- 2 cups French vanilla coffee creamer
- 1 tablespoon agave nectar
- 2 ounces vodka
- 1 tablespoon rainbow sprinkles

Preparation:

1. In an empty Ninja CREAMi pint container, place all ingredients and mix well.
2. Cover the container with storage lid and freeze for 24 hours.
3. After 24 hours, remove the lid from container and arrange into the Outer Bowl of Ninja CREAMi.
4. Install the Creamerizer Paddle onto the lid of Outer Bowl.
5. Then rotate the lid clockwise to lock.
6. Press Power button to turn on the unit.
7. Then press Milkshake button.
8. When the program is completed, turn the Outer Bowl and release it from the machine.
9. Transfer the shake into serving glasses and serve immediately.

Serving Suggestions: Serve with the topping of extra sprinkles.

Variation Tip: For more flavor, use vanilla vodka.

Nutritional Information per Serving:
Calories: 563| Fat: 46.3g|Sat Fat: 28.9g|Carbohydrates: 16.8g| Fiber: 0.5g|Sugar: 7.8g|Protein: 6.5g

Marshmallow Milkshake

Preparation Time: 10 minutes
Servings: 2

Ingredients:

- 1½ cups vanilla ice cream
- ½ cup oat milk
- ½ cup marshmallow cereal

Preparation:

1. In an empty Ninja CREAMi pint container, place ice cream followed by oat milk and marshmallow cereal.
2. Arrange the container into the Outer Bowl of Ninja CREAMi.
3. Install the Creamerizer Paddle onto the lid of Outer Bowl.
4. Then rotate the lid clockwise to lock.
5. Press Power button to turn on the unit.
6. Then press Milkshake button.
7. When the program is completed, turn the Outer Bowl and release it from the machine.
8. Transfer the shake into serving glasses and serve immediately.

Serving Suggestions: Serve with the topping of mini marshmallows.

Variation Tip: Feel free to use milk of your choice.

Nutritional Information per Serving:
Calories: 165 | Fat: 6.1g|Sat Fat: 3.5g|Carbohydrates: 24.8g| Fiber: 1.1g|Sugar: 19.3g|Protein: 3g

Lemon Cookie Milkshake

Preparation Time: 10 minutes
Servings: 2

Ingredients:

- 1½ cups vanilla ice cream
- 3 lemon cream sandwich cookies
- ¼ cup milk

Preparation:

1. In an empty Ninja CREAMi pint container, place ice cream followed by cookies and milk.
2. Arrange the container into the Outer Bowl of Ninja CREAMi.
3. Install the Creamerizer Paddle onto the lid of Outer Bowl.
4. Then rotate the lid clockwise to lock.
5. Press Power button to turn on the unit.
6. Then press Milkshake button.
7. When the program is completed, turn the Outer Bowl and release it from the machine.
8. Transfer the shake into serving glasses and serve immediately.

Serving Suggestions: Serve with the sprinkling of cinnamon.

Variation Tip: Don't use skim milk in this recipe.

Nutritional Information per Serving:
Calories: 222 | Fat: 10g|Sat Fat: 5.3g|Carbohydrates: 29.1g| Fiber: 1.4g|Sugar: 21.3g|Protein: 3.8g

Pecan Milkshake

Preparation Time: 10 minutes
Servings: 2

Ingredients:

- 1½ cups vanilla ice cream
- ½ cup unsweetened soy milk
- 2 tablespoons maple syrup
- ¼ cup pecans, chopped
- 1 teaspoon ground cinnamon
- Pinch of salt

Preparation:

1. In an empty Ninja CREAMi pint container, place ice cream followed by soy milk, maple syrup, pecans, cinnamon and salt.
2. Arrange the container into the Outer Bowl of Ninja CREAMi.
3. Install the Creamerizer Paddle onto the lid of Outer Bowl.
4. Then rotate the lid clockwise to lock.
5. Press Power button to turn on the unit.
6. Then press Milkshake button.
7. When the program is completed, turn the Outer Bowl and release it from the machine.
8. Transfer the shake into serving glasses and serve immediately.

Serving Suggestions: Serve with the topping of extra pecans.

Variation Tip: Maple syrup can be replaced with honey.

Nutritional Information per Serving:
Calories: 309 | Fat: 18.5g|Sat Fat: 4.7g|Carbohydrates: 32.6g|Fiber: 3.2g|Sugar: 25.5g|Protein: 5.6g

Banana Milkshake

Preparation Time: 10 minutes
Servings: 2

Ingredients:

- 1 scoop vanilla ice cream
- 2 small bananas, peeled and halved
- 7 fluid ounces semi-skimmed milk

Preparation:

1. In an empty Ninja CREAMi pint container, place ice cream followed by bananas and milk.
2. Arrange the container into the Outer Bowl of Ninja CREAMi.
3. Install the Creamerizer Paddle onto the lid of Outer Bowl.
4. Then rotate the lid clockwise to lock.
5. Press Power button to turn on the unit.
6. Then press Milkshake button.
7. When the program is completed, turn the Outer Bowl and release it from the machine.
8. Transfer the shake into serving glasses and serve immediately.

Serving Suggestions: Serve with the sprinkling of ground cinnamon.

Variation Tip: You can use non-dairy milk in this recipe.

Nutritional Information per Serving:
Calories: 210 | Fat: 4.9g|Sat Fat: 2.4g|Carbohydrates: 36.3g|Fiber: 2.9g|Sugar: 19.4g|Protein: 5.4g

Mixed Berries Milkshake

Preparation Time: 10 minutes
Servings: 2

Ingredients:

- 1½ cups vanilla ice cream
- ½ cup milk
- ½ cup fresh mixed berries

Preparation:

1. In an empty Ninja CREAMi pint container, place ice cream followed by milk and berries.
2. Arrange the container into the outer bowl of Ninja CREAMi.
3. Install the Creamerizer Paddle onto the lid of Outer Bowl.
4. Then rotate the lid clockwise to lock.
5. Press Power button to turn on the unit.
6. Then press Milkshake button.
7. When the program is completed, turn the Outer Bowl and release it from the machine.
8. Transfer the shake into serving glasses and serve immediately.

Serving Suggestions: Serve with garnishing of fresh berries.

Variation Tip: You can also use strawberry ice cream in this recipe

Nutritional Information per Serving:
Calories: 153 | Fat: 6.6g|Sat Fat: 4.1g|Carbohydrates: 19.3g|Fiber: 1.6g|Sugar: 15.8g|Protein: 4g

Chocolate Yogurt Milkshake

Preparation Time: 10 minutes
Servings: 2

Ingredients:

- 1 cup frozen chocolate yogurt
- 1 scoop chocolate whey protein powder
- 1 cup whole milk

Preparation:

1. In an empty Ninja CREAMi pint container, place yogurt followed by protein powder and milk.
2. Arrange the container into the Outer Bowl of Ninja CREAMi.
3. Install the Creamerizer Paddle onto the lid of Outer Bowl.
4. Then rotate the lid clockwise to lock.
5. Press Power button to turn on the unit.
6. Then press Milkshake button.
7. When the program is completed, turn the Outer Bowl and release it from the machine.
8. Transfer the shake into serving glasses and serve immediately.

Serving Suggestions: Serve with the topping of whipped cream.

Variation Tip: use high-quality protein powder.

Nutritional Information per Serving:
Calories: 242 | Fat: 4.8g|Sat Fat: 2.8g|Carbohydrates: 30.7g|Fiber: 0.4g|Sugar: 27.5g|Protein: 18.6g

Chocolate Ice Cream Milkshake

Preparation Time: 10 minutes
Servings: 1

Ingredients:

- 1½ cups chocolate ice cream
- ½ cup whole milk

Preparation:

1. In an empty Ninja CREAMi pint container, place ice cream, followed by milk.
2. Arrange the container into the Outer Bowl of Ninja CREAMi.
3. Install the Creamerizer Paddle onto the lid of Outer Bowl.
4. Then rotate the lid clockwise to lock.
5. Press Power button to turn on the unit.
6. Then press Milkshake button.
7. When the program is completed, turn the Outer Bowl and release it from the machine.
8. Transfer the shake into a serving glass and serve immediately.

Serving Suggestions: Serve with the drizzling of maple syrup.

Variation Tip: Don't use non-dairy milk in this recipe.

Nutritional Information per Serving:
Calories: 279 | Fat: 14.5g|Sat Fat: 9g|Carbohydrates: 29.5g|Fiber: 0.8g|Sugar: 27.4g|Protein: 7.4g

Chocolate Cherry Milkshake

Preparation Time: 10 minutes
Servings: 2

Ingredients:

- 1½ cups chocolate ice cream
- ½ cup canned cherries in syrup, drained
- ¼ cup whole milk

Preparation:

1. In an empty Ninja CREAMi pint container, place ice cream followed by cherries and milk.
2. Arrange the container into the Outer Bowl of Ninja CREAMi.
3. Install the Creamerizer Paddle onto the lid of Outer Bowl.
4. Then rotate the lid clockwise to lock.
5. Press Power button to turn on the unit.
6. Then press Milkshake button.
7. When the program is completed, turn the Outer Bowl and release it from the machine.
8. Transfer the shake into serving glasses and serve immediately.

Serving Suggestions: Serve with the garnishing of mascarpone cherries.

Variation Tip: For best result use canned cherries.

Nutritional Information per Serving:
Calories: 143 | Fat: 6.3g|Sat Fat: 4g|Carbohydrates: 18.8g|Fiber: 1.1g|Sugar: 16.7g|Protein: 3.2g

Cashew Butter Milkshake

Preparation Time: 10 minutes
Servings: 2

Ingredients:

- 1½ cups vanilla ice cream
- ½ cup canned cashew milk
- ¼ cup cashew butter

Preparation:

1. In an empty Ninja CREAMi pint container, place the ice cream.
2. With a spoon, create a 1½-inch wide hole in the center that reaches the bottom of the pint container.
3. Add the remaining ingredients into the hole.
4. Arrange the container into the Outer Bowl of Ninja CREAMi.
5. Install the Creamerizer Paddle onto the lid of Outer Bowl.
6. Then rotate the lid clockwise to lock.
7. Press Power button to turn on the unit.
8. Then press Milkshake button.
9. When the program is completed, turn the Outer Bowl and release it from the machine.
10. Transfer the shake into serving glasses and serve immediately.

Serving Suggestions: Serve with topping of chopped cashews.

Variation Tip: Full-fat coconut milk can be also used instead of cashew milk.

Nutritional Information per Serving:
Calories: 297 | Fat: 21.6g|Sat Fat: 6.5g|Carbohydrates: 21.1g|Fiber: 1g|Sugar: 10.5g|Protein: 7.4g

Cacao Mint Milkshake

Preparation Time: 10 minutes
Servings: 2

Ingredients:

- 1½ cups vanilla ice cream
- ½ cup canned full-fat coconut milk
- 1 teaspoon matcha powder
- ¼ cup cacao nibs
- 1 teaspoon peppermint extract

Preparation:

1. In an empty Ninja CREAMi pint container, place ice cream followed by coconut milk, matcha powder, cacao nibs and peppermint extract.
2. Arrange the container into the Outer Bowl of Ninja CREAMi.
3. Install the Creamerizer Paddle onto the lid of Outer Bowl.
4. Then rotate the lid clockwise to lock.
5. Press Power button to turn on the unit.
6. Then press Milkshake button.
7. When the program is completed, turn the Outer Bowl and release it from the machine.
8. Transfer the shake into serving glasses and serve immediately.

Serving Suggestions: Serve with the topping crushed chocolate cookies.

Variation Tip: use high quality cacao nibs.

Nutritional Information per Serving:
Calories: 363 | Fat: 26.2g|Sat Fat: 19.7g|Carbohydrates: 26.8g|Fiber: 4.8g|Sugar: 19.8g|Protein: 5.4g

Mocha Milkshake

Preparation Time: 10 minutes
Servings: 2

Ingredients:

- 1½ cups chocolate ice cream
- ½ cup cashew milk
- ½ cup ripe banana, peeled and cut into ½-inch pieces
- 1 tablespoon instant coffee powder

Preparation:

1. In an empty Ninja CREAMi pint container, place ice cream followed by milk, banana and coffee powder.
2. Arrange the container into the Outer Bowl of Ninja CREAMi.
3. Install the Creamerizer Paddle onto the lid of Outer Bowl.
4. Then rotate the lid clockwise to lock.
5. Press Power button to turn on the unit.
6. Then press Milkshake button.
7. When the program is completed, turn the Outer Bowl and release it from the machine.
8. Transfer the shake into serving glasses and serve immediately.

Serving Suggestions: Serve with the topping of chocolate shaving.

Variation Tip: Make sure to use ripe banana.

Nutritional Information per Serving:
Calories: 142 | Fat: 5.9g|Sat Fat: 3.4g|Carbohydrates: 20.8g|Fiber: 1.4g|Sugar: 15.1g|Protein: 2.2g

Mocha Tahini Milkshake

Preparation Time: 10 minutes
Servings: 2

Ingredients:

- 1½ cups chocolate ice cream
- ½ cup unsweetened oat milk
- ¼ cup tahini
- 2 tablespoons coffee
- 1 tablespoon chocolate fudge

Preparation:

1. In an empty Ninja CREAMi pint container, place ice cream followed by milk, tahini, coffee and fudge.
2. Arrange the container into the Outer Bowl of Ninja CREAMi.
3. Install the Creamerizer Paddle onto the lid of Outer Bowl.
4. Then rotate the lid clockwise to lock.
5. Press Power button to turn on the unit.
6. Then press Milkshake button.
7. When the program is completed, turn the Outer Bowl and release it from the machine.
8. Transfer the shake into serving glasses and serve immediately.

Serving Suggestions: Serve with the topping of whipped cream.

Variation Tip: You can use milk of your choice.

Nutritional Information per Serving:
Calories: 174 | Fat: 11.4g|Sat Fat: 3g|Carbohydrates: 15.2g|Fiber: 2g|Sugar: 9.5g|Protein: 4.1g

Coffee Smoothie Bowl

Preparation Time: 10 minutes
Servings: 2

Ingredients:

- 2 cups unsweetened vanilla almond milk
- ¼ cup instant coffee

Preparation:

1. In a large bowl, add the almond milk and instant coffee mix and beat until well combine
2. Transfer the mixture into an empty Ninja CREAMi pint container.
3. Cover the container with storage lid and freeze for 24 hours.
4. After 24 hours, remove the lid from container and arrange into the Outer Bowl of Ninja CREAMi.
5. Install the Creamerizer Paddle onto the lid of Outer Bowl.
6. Then rotate the lid clockwise to lock.
7. Press Power button to turn on the unit.
8. Then press Smoothie Bowl button.
9. When the program is completed, turn the Outer Bowl and release it from the machine.
10. Transfer the smoothie into serving bowls and serve immediately.

Serving Suggestions: Serve with the topping of banana, almonds, coconut and chocolate chips.

Variation Tip: You can use plain almond milk.

Nutritional Information per Serving:
Calories: 40 | Fat: 3.5g|Sat Fat: 0.3g|Carbohydrates: 2g|Fiber: 1g|Sugar: 0g|Protein: 1g

Oat Banana Smoothie Bowl

Preparation Time: 10 minutes
Cooking Time: 1 minute
Servings: 2

Ingredients:

- ½ cup water
- ¼ cup quick oats
- 1 cup vanilla Greek yogurt
- ½ cup banana, peeled and sliced
- 3 tablespoons honey

Preparation:

1. In a small microwave-safe bowl, add the water and oats and microwave on High or about one minute.
2. Remove from the microwave and stir in the yogurt, banana and honey until well combined.
3. Transfer the mixture into an empty Ninja CREAMi pint container.
4. Cover the container with storage lid and freeze for 24 hours.
5. After 24 hours, remove the lid from container and arrange into the Outer Bowl of Ninja CREAMi.
6. Install the Creamerizer Paddle onto the lid of Outer Bowl.
7. Then rotate the lid clockwise to lock.
8. Press Power button to turn on the unit.
9. Then press Smoothie Bowl button.
10. When the program is completed, turn the Outer Bowl and release it from the machine.
11. Transfer the smoothie into serving bowls and serve with your favorite topping.

Serving Suggestions: Serve with the topping of banana, granola and nuts.

Variation Tip: You can use plain yogurt too.

Nutritional Information per Serving:
Calories: 278 | Fat: 2.7g|Sat Fat: 1.1g|Carbohydrates: 55.7g|Fiber: 2.1g|Sugar: 41.6g|Protein: 10.9g

Strawberry Smoothie Bowl

Preparation Time: 10 minutes
Servings: 4

Ingredients:

- 2 tablespoons vanilla protein powder
- ¼ cup agave nectar
- ¼ cup pineapple juice
- ½ cup whole milk
- 1 cup ripe banana, peeled and cut in ½-inch pieces
- 1 cup fresh strawberries, hulled and quartered

Preparation:

1. In a large bowl, add the protein powder, agave nectar, pineapple juice and milk and beat until well combined.
2. Place the banana and strawberry into an empty Ninja CREAMi pint container and with the back of a spoon, firmly press the fruit below the Max Fill line.
3. Top with milk mixture and mix until well combined.
4. Cover the container with storage lid and freeze for 24 hours.
5. After 24 hours, remove the lid from container and arrange into the Outer Bowl of Ninja CREAMi.
6. Install the Creamerizer Paddle onto the lid of Outer Bowl.
7. Then rotate the lid clockwise to lock.
8. Press Power button to turn on the unit.
9. Then press Smoothie Bowl button.
10. When the program is completed, turn the Outer Bowl and release it from the machine.
11. Transfer the smoothie into serving bowls and serve immediately.

Serving Suggestions: Serve with the topping of fresh strawberry slices, coconut and chocolate shaving.

Variation Tip: You can adjust the ratio of sweetener according to your taste.

Nutritional Information per Serving:
Calories: 145 | Fat: 1.3g|Sat Fat: 0.6g|Carbohydrates: 31g|Fiber: 2.7g|Sugar: 24.7g|Protein: 4.7g

Raspberry Smoothie Bowl

Preparation Time: 10 minutes
Servings: 4

Ingredients:

- 1 cup brewed coffee
- ½ cup oat milk
- 2 tablespoons almond butter
- 1 cup fresh raspberries
- 1 large banana, peeled and sliced

Preparation:

1. In a high-speed blender add all the ingredients and pulse until smooth.
2. Transfer the mixture into an empty Ninja CREAMi pint container.
3. Cover the container with storage lid and freeze for 24 hours.
4. After 24 hours, remove the lid from container and arrange into the Outer Bowl of Ninja CREAMi.
5. Install the Creamerizer Paddle onto the lid of Outer Bowl.
6. Then rotate the lid clockwise to lock.
7. Press Power button to turn on the unit.
8. Then press Smoothie Bowl button.
9. When the program is completed, turn the Outer Bowl and release it from the machine.
10. Transfer the smoothie into serving bowls and serve immediately.

Serving Suggestions: Serve with the topping of berries, coconut and granola.

Variation Tip: Cashew butter can be used instead of almond butter.

Nutritional Information per Serving:
Calories: 108 | Fat: 5.1g|Sat Fat: 0.4g|Carbohydrates: 14.9g|Fiber: 3.8g|Sugar: 7.7g|Protein: 3g

Mixed Berries Smoothie Bowl

Preparation Time: 10 minutes
Servings: 4

Ingredients:

- ¾ cup fresh strawberries, hulled and quartered
- ¾ cup fresh raspberries
- ¾ cup fresh blueberries
- ¾ cup fresh blackberries
- ¼ cup plain Greek yogurt
- 1 tablespoon honey

Preparation:

1. In an empty Ninja CREAMi pint container, place the berries and with the back of a spoon, firmly press the berries below the Max Fill line.
2. Add the yogurt and honey and stir to combine.
3. Cover the container with storage lid and freeze for 24 hours.
4. After 24 hours, remove the lid from container and arrange into the Outer Bowl of Ninja CREAMi.
5. Install the Creamerizer Paddle onto the lid of Outer Bowl.
6. Then rotate the lid clockwise to lock.
7. Press Power button to turn on the unit.
8. Then press Smoothie Bowl button.
9. When the program is completed, turn the Outer Bowl and release it from the machine.
10. Transfer the smoothie into serving bowls and serve immediately.

Serving Suggestions: Serve with the topping of berries, coconut and granola.

Variation Tip: You can use flavored yogurt in this recipe.

Nutritional Information per Serving:
Calories: 104 | Fat: 0.5g|Sat Fat: 0g|Carbohydrates: 18.7g|Fiber: 4.1g|Sugar: 13.7g|Protein: 8.6g

Berries & Cherry Smoothie Bowl

Preparation Time: 10 minutes
Servings: 4

Ingredients:

- 1 cup cranberry juice cocktail
- ¼ cup agave nectar
- 2 cups frozen cherry berry blend

Preparation:

1. In a large bowl, add the agave nectar and cranberry juice cocktail and beat until well combined.
2. Place the cherry berry blend into an empty Ninja CREAMi pint container.
3. Top with cocktail mixture and stir to combine.
4. Cover the container with storage lid and freeze for 24 hours.
5. After 24 hours, remove the lid from container and arrange into the Outer Bowl of Ninja CREAMi.
6. Install the Creamerizer Paddle onto the lid of outer bowl.
7. Then rotate the lid clockwise to lock.
8. Press Power button to turn on the unit.
9. Then press Smoothie Bowl button.
10. When the program is completed, turn the Outer Bowl and release it from the machine.
11. Transfer the smoothie into serving bowls and serve immediately.

Serving Suggestions: Serve with the topping of berries and nuts.

Variation Tip: Agave nectar can be replaced with honey.

Nutritional Information per Serving:
Calories: 127 | Fat: 0.3g|Sat Fat: 0g|Carbohydrates: 1.5g|Fiber: 2.5g|Sugar: 27.5g|Protein: 0.5g
fresh berries, oats

Pineapple Smoothie Bowl

Preparation Time: 10 minutes
Servings: 4

Ingredients:

- 2 ripe bananas, peeled and cut in 1-inch pieces
- 1 cup fresh pineapple, chopped
- ¼ cup yogurt
- 2 tablespoons honey

Preparation:

1. In a large bowl, add all the ingredients and beat until well combined.
2. Transfer the mixture into an empty Ninja CREAMi pint container.
3. Cover the container with storage lid and freeze for 24 hours.
4. After 24 hours, remove the lid from container and arrange into the Outer Bowl of Ninja CREAMi.
5. Install the Creamerizer Paddle onto the lid of Outer Bowl.
6. Then rotate the lid clockwise to lock.
7. Press Power button to turn on the unit.
8. Then press Smoothie Bowl button.
9. When the program is completed, turn the Outer Bowl and release it from the machine.
10. Transfer the smoothie into serving bowls and serve immediately.

Serving Suggestions: Serve with the topping of fresh peaches and almonds.

Variation Tip: You can use flavored yogurt in this recipe.

Nutritional Information per Serving:
Calories: 116 | Fat: 0.4g|Sat Fat: 0.2g|Carbohydrates: 28.6g|Fiber: 2.1g|Sugar: 21g|Protein: 1.8g

Mango Smoothie Bowl

Preparation Time: 10 minutes
Servings: 4

Ingredients:

- 2 cups ripe mango, peeled, pitted and cut into 1-inch pieces
- 1 (14-ounces) can of unsweetened coconut milk

Preparation:

1. Place the mango pieces into an empty Ninja CREAMi pint container.
2. Top with coconut milk and stir to combine.
3. Cover the container with storage lid and freeze for 24 hours.
4. After 24 hours, remove the lid from container and arrange into the Outer Bowl of Ninja CREAMi.
5. Install the Creamerizer Paddle onto the lid of Outer Bowl.
6. Then rotate the lid clockwise to lock.
7. Press Power button to turn on the unit.
8. Then press Smoothie Bowl button.
9. When the program is completed, turn the Outer Bowl and release it from the machine.
10. Transfer the smoothie into serving bowls and serve immediately.

Serving Suggestions: Serve with the topping of fresh fruit and coconut.

Variation Tip: You can drizzle this smoothie bowl with some honey.

Nutritional Information per Serving:
Calories: 198 | Fat: 14g|Sat Fat: 12.5g|Carbohydrates: 14.8g|Fiber: 1.3g|Sugar: 13.8g|Protein: 1.g

Mango & Raspberry Smoothie Bowl

Preparation Time: 10 minutes
Servings: 2

Ingredients:

- ¾ cup frozen mango chunks
- ½ cup frozen raspberries
- ½ cup whole milk Greek yogurt
- 2 tablespoons avocado flesh
- 1 tablespoon agave nectar

Preparation:

1. In a large bowl, add all the ingredients and mix well.
2. Transfer the mixture into an empty Ninja CREAMi pint container.
3. Cover the container with storage lid and freeze for 24 hours.
4. After 24 hours, remove the lid from container and arrange into the Outer Bowl of Ninja CREAMi.
5. Install the Creamerizer Paddle onto the lid of Outer Bowl.
6. Then rotate the lid clockwise to lock.
7. Press Power button to turn on the unit.
8. Then press Smoothie Bowl button.
9. When the program is completed, turn the Outer Bowl and release it from the machine.
10. Transfer the smoothie into serving bowls and serve immediately.

Serving Suggestions: Serve with the topping of mango, raspberries and coconut.

Variation Tip: Use flesh of ripe avocado.

Nutritional Information per Serving:
Calories: 163 | Fat: 5g|Sat Fat: 3.5g|Carbohydrates: 27.4g|Fiber: 3.5g|Sugar: 23.4g|Protein: 3.9g

Mango & Orange Smoothie Bowl

Preparation Time: 10 minutes
Servings: 2

Ingredients:

- 1 cup frozen mango chunks
- 1 cup plain whole milk yogurt
- ¼ cup fresh orange juice
- 2 tablespoons maple syrup
- ½ teaspoon ground turmeric
- 1/8 teaspoon ground cinnamon
- 1/8 teaspoon ground ginger
- Pinch of ground black pepper

Preparation:

1. In a high-speed blender, add all ingredients and pulse until smooth
2. Transfer the mixture into an empty Ninja CREAMi pint container.
3. Cover the container with storage lid and freeze for 24 hours.
4. After 24 hours, remove the lid from container and arrange into the Outer Bowl of Ninja CREAMi.
5. Install the Creamerizer Paddle onto the lid of Outer Bowl.
6. Then rotate the lid clockwise to lock.
7. Press Power button to turn on the unit.
8. Then press Smoothie Bowl button.
9. When the program is completed, turn the Outer Bowl and release it from the machine.
10. Transfer the smoothie into serving bowls and serve immediately.

Serving Suggestions: Serve with the toping of fresh fruit and coconut.

Variation Tip: For best result, use freshly squeezed orange juice.

Nutritional Information per Serving:
Calories: 188 | Fat: 4.2g|Sat Fat: 2.5g|Carbohydrates: 34.8g|Fiber: 1.5g|Sugar: 31.1g|Protein: 4.9g

Dragon Fruit & Pineapple Smoothie Bowl

Preparation Time: 10 minutes
Servings: 4

Ingredients:

- 2 cups frozen dragon fruit chunks
- 2 (6-ounces) cans pineapple juice

Preparation:

1. Place the dragon fruit chunks into an empty Ninja CREAMi pint container.
2. Top with pineapple juice and stir to combine.
3. Cover the container with storage lid and freeze for 24 hours.
4. After 24 hours, remove the lid from container and arrange into the Outer Bowl of Ninja CREAMi.
5. Install the Creamerizer Paddle onto the lid of Outer Bowl.
6. Then rotate the lid clockwise to lock.
7. Press Power button to turn on the unit.
8. Then press Smoothie Bowl button.
9. When the program is completed, turn the Outer Bowl and release it from the machine.
10. Transfer the smoothie into serving bowls and serve immediately.

Serving Suggestions: Serve with the topping of fruit, chia seeds and granola.

Variation Tip: If you like sweeter smoothie, then use some sweetener.

Nutritional Information per Serving:
Calories: 68 | Fat: 0.1g|Sat Fat: 0g|Carbohydrates: 17g|Fiber: 0.2g|Sugar: 14.5g|Protein: 0.3g

Pumpkin Smoothie Bowl

Preparation Time: 10 minutes
Servings: 2

Ingredients:

- 1 cup canned pumpkin puree
- ⅓ cup plain Greek yogurt
- 1½ tablespoons maple syrup
- 1 teaspoon vanilla extract
- 1 teaspoon pumpkin pie spice
- 1 frozen banana, peeled and cut in ½-inch pieces

Preparation:

1. In an empty Ninja CREAMi pint container, add the pumpkin puree, yogurt, maple syrup, vanilla extract and pumpkin pie spice and mix well.
2. Add the banana pieces and stir to combine.
3. Transfer the mixture into an empty Ninja CREAMi pint container.
4. Arrange the container into the Outer Bowl of Ninja CREAMi.
5. Install the Creamerizer Paddle onto the lid of Outer Bowl.
6. Then rotate the lid clockwise to lock.
7. Press Power button to turn on the unit.
8. Then press Smoothie Bowl button.
9. When the program is completed, turn the Outer Bowl and release it from the machine.
10. Transfer the smoothie into serving bowls and serve immediately.

Serving Suggestions: Serve with garnishing of pumpkin seeds and chocolate chips.

Variation Tip: Use sugar-free pumpkin puree.

Nutritional Information per Serving:
Calories: 170 | Fat: 0.7g|Sat Fat: 0.3g|Carbohydrates: 35.8g|Fiber: 5.2g|Sugar: 22g|Protein: 7.5g

Kale, Avocado & fruit Smoothie Bowl

Preparation Time: 10 minutes
Servings: 4

Ingredients:

- 1 banana, peeled and cut into 1-inch pieces
- ½ of avocado, peeled, pitted and cut into 1-inch pieces
- 1 cup fresh kale leaves
- 1 cup green apple, peeled, cored and cut into 1-inch pieces
- ¼ cup unsweetened coconut milk
- 2 tablespoons agave nectar

Preparation:

1. In a large high-speed blender, add all the ingredients and pulse until smooth.
2. Transfer the mixture into an empty Ninja CREAMi pint container.
3. Cover the container with storage lid and freeze for 24 hours.
4. After 24 hours, remove the lid from container and arrange into the Outer Bowl of Ninja CREAMi.
5. Install the Creamerizer Paddle onto the lid of Outer Bowl.
6. Then rotate the lid clockwise to lock.
7. Press Power button to turn on the unit.
8. Then press Smoothie Bowl button.
9. When the program is completed, turn the Outer Bowl and release it from the machine.
10. Transfer the smoothie into serving bowls and serve immediately.

Serving Suggestions: Serve with the topping of fresh berries and coconut.

Variation Tip: Kale can be replaced with spinach.

Nutritional Information per Serving:
Calories: 179 | Fat: 8.7g|Sat Fat: 4.2g|Carbohydrates: 27.2g|Fiber: 4.9g|Sugar: 17.5g|Protein: 1.8g

Matcha Ice Cream

Preparation Time: 15 minutes
Cooking Time: 10 seconds
Servings: 4

Ingredients:

- 1 tablespoon cream cheese, softened
- ⅓ cup granulated sugar
- 2 tablespoons matcha powder
- 1 teaspoon vanilla extract
- 1 cup whole milk
- ¾ cup heavy cream

Preparation:

1. In a large microwave-safe bowl, add the cream cheese and microwave for on High for about ten seconds.
2. Remove from the microwave and stir until smooth.
3. Add the sugar, matcha powder and vanilla extract and with a wire whisk, beat until the mixture looks like frosting.
4. Slowly add the milk and heavy cream and beat until well combined.
5. Transfer the mixture into an empty Ninja CREAMi pint container.
6. Cover the container with storage lid and freeze for 24 hours.
7. After 24 hours, remove the lid from container and arrange into the Outer Bowl of Ninja CREAMi.
8. Install the Creamerizer Paddle onto the lid of Outer Bowl.
9. Then rotate the lid clockwise to lock.
10. Press Power button to turn on the unit.
11. Then press Ice Cream button.
12. When the program is completed, turn the Outer Bowl and release it from the machine.
13. Transfer the ice cream into serving bowls and serve immediately.

Serving Suggestions: Serve with the topping of chopped nuts.

Variation Tip: You can use almond extract instead of vanilla extract.

Nutritional Information per Serving:
Calories: 188 | Fat: 11.2g|Sat Fat: 6.9g|Carbohydrates: 20.3g|Fiber: 0g|Sugar: 20g|Protein: 2.6g

Earl Grey Tea Ice Cream

Preparation Time: 15 minutes
Cooking Time: 25 minutes
Servings: 4

Ingredients:

- 1 cup heavy cream
- 1 cup whole milk
- 5 tablespoons monk fruit sweetener
- 3 Earl Grey tea bags

Preparation:

1. In a medium saucepan, add cream and milk and stir to combine.
2. Place saucepan over medium heat and cook until for bout two-three minutes or until steam is rising.
3. Stir in the monk fruit sweetener and reduce the heat to very low.
4. Add teabags and cover the saucepan for about 20 minutes.
5. Discard the tea bags and remove saucepan from heat.
6. Transfer the mixture into an empty Ninja CREAMi pint container and place into an ice bath to cool.
7. After cooling, cover the container with storage lid and freeze for 24 hours.
8. After 24 hours, remove the lid from container and arrange into the Outer Bowl of Ninja CREAMi.
9. Install the Creamerizer Paddle onto the lid of Outer Bowl.
10. Then rotate the lid clockwise to lock.
11. Press Power button to turn on the unit.
12. Then press Ice Cream button.
13. When the program is completed, turn the Outer Bowl and release it from the machine.
14. Transfer the ice cream into serving bowls and serve immediately.

Serving Suggestions: Serve with the garnishing of chocolate chips.

Variation Tip: You can use your favorite sweetener instead of monk fruit sweetener.

Nutritional Information per Serving:
Calories: 140 | Fat: 13.1g|Sat Fat: 8.1g|Carbohydrates: 3.6g|Fiber: 0g|Sugar: 3.2g|Protein: 2.6g

Fruity Extract Ice Cream

Preparation Time: 10 minutes
Servings: 4

Ingredients:

- 1 cup whole milk
- ¾ cup heavy cream
- 2 tablespoons monk fruit sweetener with Erythritol
- 2 tablespoons agave nectar
- ½ teaspoon raspberry extract
- ½ teaspoon vanilla extract
- ¼ teaspoon lemon extract
- 5-6 drops blue food coloring

Preparation:

1. In a bowl, add all ingredients and eat until well combined.
2. Transfer the mixture into an empty Ninja CREAMi pint container.
3. Cover the container with storage lid and freeze for 24 hours.
4. After 24 hours, remove the lid from container and arrange into the Outer Bowl of Ninja CREAMi.
5. Install the Creamerizer Paddle onto the lid of outer bowl.
6. Then rotate the lid clockwise to lock.
7. Press Power button to turn on the unit.
8. Then press Ice Cream button.
9. When the program is completed, turn the Outer Bowl and release it from the machine.
10. Transfer the ice cream into serving bowls and serve immediately.

Serving Suggestions: Serve with the topping of fresh fruit.

Variation Tip: Use organic food coloring.

Nutritional Information per Serving:
Calories: 147 | Fat: 10.3g|Sat Fat: 6.3g|Carbohydrates: 11.6g|Fiber: 0.6g|Sugar: 10.9g|Protein: 2.4g

Peanut Butter Ice Cream

Preparation Time: 10 minutes
Servings: 4

Ingredients:

- 1¾ cups skim milk
- 3 tablespoons smooth peanut butter
- ¼ cup stevia-cane sugar blend
- 1 teaspoon vanilla extract

Preparation:

1. In a bowl, add all ingredients and beat until smooth.
2. Set aside for about five minutes.
3. Transfer the mixture into an empty Ninja CREAMi pint container.
4. Cover the container with storage lid and freeze for 24 hours.
5. After 24 hours, remove the lid from container and arrange into the outer bowl of Ninja CREAMi.
6. Install the Creamerizer Paddle onto the lid of Outer Bowl.
7. Then rotate the lid clockwise to lock.
8. Press Power button to turn on the unit.
9. Then press Ice Cream button.
10. When the program is completed, turn the Outer Bowl and release it from the machine.
11. Transfer the ice cream into serving bowls and serve immediately.

Serving Suggestions: Serve with topping of white chocolate chips.

Variation Tip: You can use milk of your choice.

Nutritional Information per Serving:
Calories: 143 | Fat: 6.1g|Sat Fat: 1.2g|Carbohydrates: 19.7g|Fiber: 0.7g|Sugar: 18.5g|Protein: 6.5g

Lemon Ice Cream

Preparation Time: 10 minutes
Servings: 4

Ingredients:

- 1 (14-ounce) can full-fat unsweetened coconut milk
- ½ cup granulated sugar
- 1 teaspoon vanilla extract
- 1 teaspoon lemon extract

Preparation:

1. In a bowl, add the coconut milk and beat until smooth.
2. Add the remaining ingredients and beat until sugar is dissolved.
3. Transfer the mixture into an empty Ninja CREAMi pint container.
4. Cover the container with storage lid and freeze for 24 hours.
5. After 24 hours, remove the lid from container and arrange into the Outer Bowl of Ninja CREAMi.
6. Install the Creamerizer Paddle onto the lid of Outer Bowl.
7. Then rotate the lid clockwise to lock.
8. Press Power button to turn on the unit.
9. Then press Ice Cream button.
10. When the program is completed, turn the Outer Bowl and release it from the machine.
11. Transfer the ice cream into serving bowls and serve immediately.

Serving Suggestions: Serve with the garnishing of sweetened whipped cream and lemon zest.

Variation Tip: Granulated sugar can be replaced with sweetener of your choice.

Nutritional Information per Serving:
Calories: 280 | Fat: 18.3g|Sat Fat: 16.8g|Carbohydrates: 28.2g|Fiber: 0g|Sugar: 26.7g|Protein: 1.5g

Pear Ice Cream

Preparation Time: 15 minutes
Cooking Time: 15 minutes
Servings: 4

Ingredients:

- 3 medium ripe pears, peeled, cored and cut into 1-inch pieces
- 1 (14-ounce) can full-fat unsweetened coconut milk
- ½ cup granulated sugar

Preparation:

1. In a medium saucepan, add all ingredients and stir to combine.
2. Place the saucepan over medium heat and bring to a boil.
3. Reduce the heat to low and simmer for about ten minutes or until liquid is reduced by half.
4. Remove from the heat and set aside to cool.
5. After cooling, transfer the mixture into a high-speed blender and pulse until smooth.
6. Transfer the mixture into an empty Ninja CREAMi pint container.
7. Cover the container with storage lid and freeze for 24 hours.
8. After 24 hours, remove the lid from container and arrange into the Outer Bowl of Ninja CREAMi.
9. Install the Creamerizer Paddle onto the lid of Outer Bowl.
10. Then rotate the lid clockwise to lock.
11. Press Power button to turn on the unit.
12. Then press Ice Cream button.
13. When the program is completed, turn the Outer Bowl and release it from the machine.
14. Transfer the ice cream into serving bowls and serve immediately.

Serving Suggestions: Serve with the drizzling of caramel syrup.

Variation Tip: Make sure to use ripe pears.

Nutritional Information per Serving:
Calories: 368 | Fat: 18.5g|Sat Fat: 168g|Carbohydrates: 51.9g|Fiber: 4.9g|Sugar: 41.8g|Protein: 2.1g

Strawberry Ice Cream

Preparation Time: 10 minutes
Servings: 4

Ingredients:

- ¼ cup sugar
- 1 tablespoon cream cheese, softened
- 1 teaspoon vanilla bean paste
- 1 cup milk
- ¾ cup heavy whipping cream
- 6 medium fresh strawberries, hulled and quartered

Preparation:

1. In a bowl, add the sugar, cream cheese, vanilla bean paste and with a wire whisk, mix until well combined.
2. Add in the milk and heavy whipping cream and beat until well combined.
3. Transfer the mixture into an empty Ninja CREAMi pint container.
4. Add the strawberry pieces and stir to combine.
5. Cover the container with storage lid and freeze for 24 hours.
6. After 24 hours, remove the lid from container and arrange into the Outer Bowl of Ninja CREAMi.
7. Install the Creamerizer Paddle onto the lid of Outer Bowl.
8. Then rotate the lid clockwise to lock.
9. Press Power button to turn on the unit.
10. Then press Ice Cream button.
11. When the program is completed, turn the Outer Bowl and release it from the machine.
12. Transfer the ice cream into serving bowls and serve immediately.

Serving Suggestions: Serve with the garnishing of chocolate wafers.

Variation Tip: Don't use frozen strawberries.

Nutritional Information per Serving:
Calories: 175 | Fat: 10.5g|Sat Fat: 6.5g|Carbohydrates: 18.8g|Fiber: 0.4g|Sugar: 17.4g|Protein: 2.8g

Blueberry Ice Cream

Preparation Time: 10 minutes
Servings: 4

Ingredients:

- 1 cup blueberries
- ½ cup vanilla whole milk Greek yogurt
- ¼ cup milk
- 2 tablespoons honey
- 2 tablespoons chia seeds

Preparation:

1. In a bowl, add all ingredients and eat until well combined.
2. Transfer the mixture into an empty Ninja CREAMi pint container.
3. Cover the container with storage lid and freeze for 24 hours.
4. After 24 hours, remove the lid from container and arrange into the Outer Bowl of Ninja CREAMi.
5. Install the Creamerizer Paddle onto the lid of Outer Bowl.
6. Then rotate the lid clockwise to lock.
7. Press Power button to turn on the unit.
8. Then press Ice Cream button.
9. When the program is completed, turn the Outer Bowl and release it from the machine.
10. Transfer the ice cream into serving bowls and serve immediately.

Serving Suggestions: Serve with the garnishing of fresh blueberries.

Variation Tip: Chia seeds can be replaced with flax seed.

Nutritional Information per Serving:
Calories: 115 | Fat: 4g|Sat Fat: 2g|Carbohydrates: 19.4g|Fiber: 2.2g|Sugar: 15.9g|Protein: 3.1g

Carrot Cheesecake Ice Cream

Preparation Time: 10 minutes
Servings: 4

Ingredients:

- 1 cup heavy cream
- ½ cup carrot juice
- ⅓ cup light brown sugar
- 2 tablespoons cream cheese frosting
- 1 teaspoon vanilla extract
- 1 teaspoon ground cinnamon

Preparation:

1. In a bowl, add all ingredients and beat until well combined.
2. Transfer the mixture into an empty Ninja CREAMi pint container.
3. Cover the container with storage lid and freeze for 24 hours.
4. After 24 hours, remove the lid from container and arrange into the Outer Bowl of Ninja CREAMi.
5. Install the Creamerizer Paddle onto the lid of Outer Bowl.
6. Then rotate the lid clockwise to lock.
7. Press Power button to turn on the unit.
8. Then press Ice Cream button.
9. When the program is completed, turn the Outer Bowl and release it from the machine.
10. Transfer the ice cream into serving bowls and serve immediately.

Serving Suggestions: Serve with the topping of chopped pecans.

Variation Tip: Use fresh carrot juice.

Nutritional Information per Serving:
Calories: 185 | Fat: 12.4g|Sat Fat: 7.3g|Carbohydrates: 18.4g|Fiber: 0.7g|Sugar: 15.8g|Protein: 0.8g

Fruit Carrot Ice Cream

Preparation Time: 15 minutes
Servings: 4

Ingredients:

- ¾ cup heavy cream
- ½ cup milk
- ⅓ cup orange juice
- ¾ cup sugar
- ¼ cup frozen carrots
- ¼ cup pineapple chunks

Preparation:

1. In a bowl, add the heavy cream, milk, orange juice and sugar and beat until sugar is dissolved.
2. In an empty Ninja CREAMi pint container, place the carrots and pineapple chunks and top with milk mixture.
3. Cover the container with storage lid and freeze for 24 hours.
4. After 24 hours, remove the lid from container and arrange into the Outer Bowl of Ninja CREAMi.
5. Install the Creamerizer Paddle onto the lid of Outer Bowl.
6. Then rotate the lid clockwise to lock.
7. Press Power button to turn on the unit.
8. Then press Ice Cream button.
9. When the program is completed, turn the Outer Bowl and release it from the machine.
10. Transfer the ice cream into serving bowls and serve immediately.

Serving Suggestions: Serve with the garnishing of orange zest.

Variation Tip: For best result, use fresh pineapple.

Nutritional Information per Serving:
Calories: 250 | Fat: 9g|Sat Fat: 5.6g|Carbohydrates: 43.5g|Fiber: 0.3g|Sugar: 41.8g|Protein: 1.7g

Coffee Ice Cream

Preparation Time: 10 minutes
Servings: 4

Ingredients:

- ¾ cup coconut cream
- ½ cup granulated sugar
- 1½ tablespoons instant coffee powder
- 1 cup rice milk
- 1 teaspoon vanilla extract

Preparation:

1. In a bowl, add coconut cream and beat until smooth.
2. Add the remaining ingredients and beat sugar is dissolved.
3. Transfer the mixture into an empty Ninja CREAMi pint container.
4. Cover the container with storage lid and freeze for 24 hours.
5. After 24 hours, remove the lid from container and arrange into the Outer Bowl of Ninja CREAMi.
6. Install the Creamerizer Paddle onto the lid of Outer Bowl.
7. Then rotate the lid clockwise to lock.
8. Press Power button to turn on the unit.
9. Then press Ice Cream button.
10. When the program is completed, turn the Outer Bowl and release it from the machine.
11. Transfer the ice cream into serving bowls and serve immediately.

Serving Suggestions: Serve with the garnishing of sweetened whipped cream.

Variation Tip: You can use almond milk too.

Nutritional Information per Serving:
Calories: 230 | Fat: 11.2g|Sat Fat: 9.6g|Carbohydrates: 33.8g|Fiber: 1g|Sugar: 26.6g|Protein: 1.1g

Mocha Ice Cream

Preparation Time: 10 minutes
Servings: 4

Ingredients:

- ½ cup mocha cappuccino mix
- 1¾ cups coconut cream
- 3 tablespoons agave nectar

Preparation:

1. In a bowl, add all ingredients and beat until well combined.
2. Transfer the mixture into an empty Ninja CREAMi pint container.
3. Cover the container with storage lid and freeze for 24 hours.
4. After 24 hours, remove the lid from container and arrange into the Outer Bowl of Ninja CREAMi.
5. Install the Creamerizer Paddle onto the lid of Outer Bowl.
6. Then rotate the lid clockwise to lock.
7. Press Power button to turn on the unit.
8. Then press Ice Cream button.
9. When the program is completed, turn the Outer Bowl and release it from the machine.
10. Transfer the ice cream into serving bowls and serve immediately.

Serving Suggestions: Serve with the garnishing of almond slices.

Variation Tip: You can use fresh cream instead of coconut cream.

Nutritional Information per Serving:
Calories: 297 | Fat: 25.4g|Sat Fat: 22.3g|Carbohydrates: 19.2g|Fiber: 3.1g|Sugar: 15.4g|Protein: 2.5g

Pistachio Ice Cream

Preparation Time: 15 minutes
Servings: 4

Ingredients:

- 1 tablespoon cream cheese, softened
- ⅓ cup granulated sugar
- 1 teaspoon almond extract
- 1 cup whole milk
- ¾ cup heavy cream
- ¼ cup pistachios, shells removed and chopped

Preparation:

1. 1n a large microwave-safe bowl, add the cream cheese and microwave on High for about ten seconds.
2. Remove from the microwave and stir until smooth.
3. Add the sugar and almond extract and with a wire whisk, beat until the mixture looks like frosting.
4. Slowly add the milk and heavy cream and beat until well combined.
5. Transfer the mixture into an empty Ninja CREAMi pint container.
6. Cover the container with storage lid and freeze for 24 hours.
7. After 24 hours, remove the lid from container and arrange into the Outer Bowl of Ninja CREAMi.
8. Install the Creamerizer Paddle onto the lid of Outer Bowl.
9. Then rotate the lid clockwise to lock.
10. Press Power button to turn on the unit.
11. Then press Ice Cream button.
12. When the program is completed, with a spoon, create a 1½-inch wide hole in the center that reaches the bottom of the pint container.
13. Add the pistachios into the hole and press Mix-In button.
14. When the program is completed, turn the Outer Bowl and release it from the machine.
15. Transfer the ice cream into serving bowls and serve immediately.

Serving Suggestions: Serve with the garnishing of pistachios.

Variation Tip: Almond extract can be replaced with vanilla extract.

Nutritional Information per Serving:
Calories: 208 | Fat: 12.9g|Sat Fat: 7.1g|Carbohydrates: 21.3g|Fiber: 0.4g|Sugar: 20.3g|Protein: 3.4g

Lavender Cookie Ice Cream

Preparation Time: 15 minutes
Cooking Time: 10 minutes
Servings: 4

Ingredients:

- ¾ cup heavy cream
- 1 tablespoon dried culinary lavender
- 1/8 teaspoon salt
- ¾ cup whole milk
- ½ cup sweetened condensed milk
- 4 drops purple food coloring
- ⅓ cup chocolate wafer cookies, crushed

Preparation:

1. In a medium saucepan, add heavy cream, lavender and salt and mix well.
2. Place the saucepan over low heat and steep, covered for about ten minutes, stirring after every two minutes.
3. Remove from the heat and through a fine-mesh strainer, strain the cream mixture into a large bowl.
4. Discard the lavender leaves.
5. In the bowl of cream mixture, add the milk, condensed milk and purple food coloring and beat until smooth.
6. Transfer the mixture into an empty Ninja CREAMi pint container.
7. Cover the container with storage lid and freeze for 24 hours.
8. After 24 hours, remove the lid from container and arrange into the Outer Bowl of Ninja CREAMi.
9. Install the Creamerizer Paddle onto the lid of Outer Bowl.
10. Then rotate the lid clockwise to lock.
11. Press Power button to turn on the unit.
12. Then press Ice Cream button.
13. When the program is completed, with a spoon, create a 1½-inch wide hole in the center that reaches the bottom of the pint container.
14. Add the crushed cookies the hole and press Mix-In button.
15. When the program is completed, turn the Outer Bowl and release it from the machine.
16. Transfer the ice cream into serving bowls and serve immediately.

Serving Suggestions: Serve with the garnishing of chocolate chunks.

Variation Tip: Use organic food color.

Nutritional Information per Serving:
Calories: 229 | Fat: 13.2g|Sat Fat: 8.1g|Carbohydrates: 23.5g|Fiber: 0g|Sugar: 23.2g|Protein: 5g

Mint Cookies Ice Cream

Preparation Time: 15 minutes
Servings: 4

Ingredients:

- ¾ cup coconut cream
- ¼ cup monk fruit sweetener with Erythritol
- 2 tablespoons agave nectar
- ½ teaspoon mint extract
- 5-6 drops green food coloring
- 1 cup oat milk
- 3 chocolate sandwich cookies, quartered

Preparation:

1. 1n a large bowl, add the coconut cream and beat until smooth.
2. Add the sweetener, agave nectar, mint extract and food coloring and beat until sweetener is dissolved.
3. Add the oat milk and beat until well combined.
4. Transfer the mixture into an empty Ninja CREAMi pint container.
5. Cover the container with storage lid and freeze for 24 hours.
6. After 24 hours, remove the lid from container and arrange into the Outer Bowl of Ninja CREAMi.
7. Install the Creamerizer Paddle onto the lid of Outer Bowl.
8. Then rotate the lid clockwise to lock.
9. Press Power button to turn on the unit.
10. Then press Lite Ice Cream button.
11. When the program is completed, with a spoon, create a 1½-inch wide hole in the center that reaches the bottom of the pint container.
12. Add the cookie pieces into the hole and press Mix-In button.
13. When the program is completed, turn the Outer Bowl and release it from the machine.
14. Transfer the ice cream into serving bowls and serve immediately.

Serving Suggestions: Serve with the garnishing of chocolate chunks.

Variation Tip: make sure to use mint extract.

Nutritional Information per Serving:
Calories: 201 | Fat: 12.8g|Sat Fat: 9.8g|Carbohydrates: 21.9g|Fiber: 2.2g|Sugar: 16.8g|Protein: 2.4g

Jelly & Peanut Butter Ice Cream

Preparation Time: 15 minutes
Cooking Time: 5 minutes
Servings: 4

Ingredients:

- 3 tablespoons granulated sugar
- 4 large egg yolks
- 1 cup whole milk
- ⅓ cup heavy cream
- ¼ cup smooth peanut butter
- 3 tablespoons grape jelly
- ¼ cup honey roasted peanuts, chopped

Preparation:

1. 1n a small saucepan, add the sugar and egg yolks and beat until sugar is dissolved.
2. Add the milk, heavy cream, peanut butter, and grape jelly to the saucepan and stir to combine.
3. Place saucepan over medium heat and cook until temperature reaches cook until temperature reaches to 165 -175° F, stirring continuously with a rubber spatula.
4. Remove from the heat and through a fine-mesh strainer, strain the mixture into an empty Ninja CREAMi pint container.
5. Place the container into ice bath to cool.
6. After cooling, cover the container with storage lid and freeze for 24 hours.
7. After 24 hours, remove the lid from container and arrange into the Outer Bowl of Ninja CREAMi.
8. Install the Creamerizer Paddle onto the lid of Outer Bowl.
9. Then rotate the lid clockwise to lock.
10. Press Power button to turn on the unit.
11. Then press ICE CREAM button.
12. When the program is completed, with a spoon, create a 1½-inch wide hole in the center that reaches the bottom of the pint container.
13. Add the peanuts into the hole and press Mix-In button.
14. When the program is completed, turn the Outer Bowl and release it from the machine.
15. Transfer the ice cream into serving bowls and serve immediately.

Serving Suggestions: Serve with the garnishing of chopped peanuts.

Variation Tip: You can use strawberry jelly instead of grape jelly.

Nutritional Information per Serving:
Calories: 349 | Fat: 23.1g|Sat Fat: 7.5g|Carbohydrates: 27.5g|Fiber: 2g|Sugar: 21.5g|Protein: 11.5g

Grasshopper Ice Cream

Preparation Time: 15 minutes
Servings: 4

Ingredients:

- ½ cup frozen spinach, thawed and squeezed dry
- 1 cup whole milk
- ½ cup granulated sugar
- 1 teaspoon mint extract
- 3-5 drops green food coloring
- ⅓ cup heavy cream
- ¼ cup chocolate chunks, chopped
- ¼ cup brownie, cut into 1-inch pieces

Preparation:

1. 1n a high-speed blender, add the spinach, milk, sugar, mint extract and food coloring and pulse until mixture smooth.
2. Transfer the mixture into an empty Ninja CREAMi pint container.
3. Add the heavy cream and stir until well combined.
4. Cover the container with storage lid and freeze for 24 hours.
5. After 24 hours, remove the lid from container and arrange into the Outer Bowl of Ninja CREAMi.
6. Install the Creamerizer Paddle onto the lid of Outer Bowl.
7. Then rotate the lid clockwise to lock.
8. Press Power button to turn on the unit.
9. Then press Ice Cream button.
10. When the program is completed, with a spoon, create a 1½-inch wide hole in the center that reaches the bottom of the pint container.
11. Add the chocolate chunks and brownie pieces into the hole and press Mix-In button.
12. When the program is completed, turn the Outer Bowl and release it from the machine.
13. Transfer the ice cream into serving bowls and serve immediately.

Serving Suggestions: Serve with the garnishing of chocolate shaving.

Variation Tip: Make sure to squeeze the spinach completely.

Nutritional Information per Serving:
Calories: 243 | Fat: 10.1g|Sat Fat: 6g|Carbohydrates: 36.7g|Fiber: 0.4g|Sugar: 33.7g|Protein: 3.4g

Snack Mix Ice Cream

Preparation Time: 15 minutes
Cooking Time: 10 seconds
Servings: 4

Ingredients:

- 1 tablespoon cream cheese, softened
- ⅓ cup granulated sugar
- ½ teaspoon vanilla extract
- 1 cup whole milk
- ¾ cup heavy cream
- 2 tablespoons sugar cone pieces
- 1 tablespoon mini pretzels
- 1 tablespoon potato chips, crushed

Preparation:

1. 1n a large microwave-safe bowl, add the cream cheese and microwave on High for about ten seconds.
2. Remove from the microwave and stir until smooth.
3. Add the sugar and vanilla extract and with a wire whisk, beat until the mixture looks like frosting.
4. Slowly add the milk and heavy cream and beat until well combined.
5. Transfer the mixture into an empty Ninja CREAMi pint container.
6. Cover the container with storage lid and freeze for 24 hours.
7. After 24 hours, remove the lid from container and arrange into the Outer Bowl of Ninja CREAMi.
8. Install the Creamerizer Paddle onto the lid of Outer Bowl.
9. Then rotate the lid clockwise to lock.
10. Press Power button to turn on the unit.
11. Then press Ice Cream button.
12. When the program is completed, with a spoon, create a 1½-inch wide hole in the center that reaches the bottom of the pint container.
13. Add the cone pieces, pretzels and potato chips into the hole and press Mix-In button.
14. When the program is completed, turn the Outer Bowl and release it from the machine.
15. Transfer the ice cream into serving bowls and serve immediately.

Serving Suggestions: Serve with the drizzling of chocolate syrup.

Variation Tip: Use full-fat cream cheese.

Nutritional Information per Serving:
Calories: 182 | Fat: 4.3g|Sat Fat: 2g|Carbohydrates: 32.8g|Fiber: 0.3g|Sugar: 23.3g|Protein: 3.6g

Coffee Chip Ice Cream

Preparation Time: 15 minutes
Servings: 4

Ingredients:

- ¾ cup heavy cream
- ¼ cup monk fruit sweetener with Erythritol
- ½ teaspoon stevia sweetener
- 1½ tablespoons instant coffee granules
- 1 cup unsweetened almond milk
- 1 teaspoon vanilla extract
- 3 tablespoons chocolate chips
- 1 tablespoon walnuts, chopped

Preparation:

1. In a bowl, add the heavy cream and beat until smooth.
2. Add the remaining ingredients except for chocolate chips and walnuts and beat sweetener is dissolved.
3. Transfer the mixture into an empty Ninja CREAMi pint container.
4. Cover the container with storage lid and freeze for 24 hours.
5. After 24 hours, remove the lid from container and arrange into the Outer Bowl of Ninja CREAMi.
6. Install the Creamerizer Paddle onto the lid of Outer Bowl.
7. Then rotate the lid clockwise to lock.
8. Press Power button to turn on the unit.
9. Then press Lite Ice Cream button.
10. When the program is completed, with a spoon, create a 1½-inch wide hole in the center that reaches the bottom of the pint container.
11. Add the chocolate chips and walnuts into the hole and press Mix-In button.
12. When the program is completed, turn the Outer Bowl and release it from the machine.
13. Transfer the ice cream into serving bowls and serve immediately.

Serving Suggestions: Serve with the garnishing of chocolate chips.

Variation Tip: Use semi-sweet chocolate chips.

Nutritional Information per Serving:
Calories: 145 | Fat: 12.7g|Sat Fat: 7g|Carbohydrates: 6.1g|Fiber: 0.7g|Sugar: 4.2g|Protein: 1.8g

Chocolate Brownie Ice Cream

Preparation Time: 14 minutes
Servings: 4

Ingredients:

- 1 tablespoon cream cheese, softened
- ⅓ cup granulated sugar
- 1 teaspoon vanilla extract
- 2 tablespoons cocoa powder
- 1 cup whole milk
- ¾ cup heavy cream
- 2 tablespoons mini chocolate chips
- 2 tablespoons brownie chunks

Preparation:

1. 1n a large microwave-safe bowl, add the cream cheese and microwave on High for about ten seconds.
2. Remove from the microwave and stir until smooth.
3. Add the sugar and almond extract and with a wire whisk, beat until the mixture looks like frosting.
4. Slowly add the milk and heavy cream and beat until well combined.
5. Transfer the mixture into an empty Ninja CREAMi pint container.
6. Cover the container with storage lid and freeze for 24 hours.
7. After 24 hours, remove the lid from container and arrange into the Outer Bowl of Ninja CREAMi.
8. Install the Creamerizer Paddle onto the lid of Outer Bowl.
9. Then rotate the lid clockwise to lock.
10. Press Power button to turn on the unit.
11. Then press Ice Cream button.
12. When the program is completed, with a spoon, create a 1½-inch wide hole in the center that reaches the bottom of the pint container.
13. Add the chocolate chunks and brownie pieces into the hole and press Mix-In button.
14. When the program is completed, turn the Outer Bowl and release it from the machine.
15. Transfer the ice cream into serving bowls and serve immediately.

Serving Suggestions: Serve with the topping of cherries.

Variation Tip: Use high-quality cocoa powder.

Nutritional Information per Serving:
Calories: 232 | Fat: 13.7g|Sat Fat: 8.3g|Carbohydrates: 25.9g|Fiber: 1g|Sugar: 22.8g|Protein: 3.6g

Rocky Road Ice Cream

Preparation Time: 15 minutes
Servings: 4

Ingredients:

- 1 cup whole milk
- ½ cup frozen cauliflower florets, thawed
- ½ cup dark brown sugar
- 3 tablespoons dark cocoa powder
- 1 teaspoon chocolate extract
- ⅓ cup heavy cream
- 2 tablespoons almonds, sliced
- 2 tablespoons mini marshmallows
- 2 tablespoons mini chocolate chips

Preparation:

1. 1n a high-speed blender, add milk, cauliflower, brown sugar, cocoa powder, and chocolate extract and pulse until smooth.
2. Transfer the mixture into an empty Ninja CREAMi pint container.
3. Add the heavy cream and stir until well combined.
4. Cover the container with storage lid and freeze for 24 hours.
5. After 24 hours, remove the lid from container and arrange into the Outer Bowl of Ninja CREAMi.
6. Install the Creamerizer Paddle onto the lid of Outer Bowl.
7. Then rotate the lid clockwise to lock.
8. Press Power button to turn on the unit.
9. Then press Ice Cream button.
10. When the program is completed, with a spoon, create a 1½-inch wide hole in the center that reaches the bottom of the pint container.
11. Add the almonds, marshmallows and chocolate chips into the hole and press Mix-In button.
12. When the program is completed, turn the Outer Bowl and release it from the machine.
13. Transfer the ice cream into serving bowls and serve immediately.

Serving Suggestions: Serve with the garnishing of marshmallows.

Variation Tip: Thaw the cauliflower florets completely.

Nutritional Information per Serving:
Calories: 202 | Fat: 9.3g|Sat Fat: 5g|Carbohydrates: 28.7g|Fiber: 2.1g|Sugar: 24.9g|Protein: 4.2g

Sorbets

60

Lime Sorbet

Preparation Time: 10 minutes
Servings: 4

Ingredients:

- ¾ cup beer
- ⅔ cup water
- ½ cup fresh lime juice
- ¼ cup granulated sugar

Preparation:

1. In a high-speed blender, add all the ingredients and pulse until smooth.
2. Set aside for about five minutes.
3. Transfer the mixture into an empty Ninja CREAMi pint container.
4. Cover the container with storage lid and freeze for 24 hours.
5. After 24 hours, remove the lid from container and arrange into the Outer Bowl of Ninja CREAMi.
6. Install the Creamerizer Paddle onto the lid of Outer Bowl.
7. Then rotate the lid clockwise to lock.
8. Press Power button to turn on the unit.
9. Then press Sorbet button.
10. When the program is completed, turn the Outer Bowl and release it from the machine.
11. Transfer the sorbet into serving bowls and serve immediately.

Serving Suggestions: Serve with the garnishing of lime zest.

Variation Tip: For best result, use canned Mexican beer.

Nutritional Information per Serving:
Calories: 69 | Fat: 0g|Sat Fat: 0g|Carbohydrates: 14.4g|Fiber: 0g|Sugar: 12.5g|Protein: 0.2g

Lemony Herb Sorbet

Preparation Time: 15 minutes
Cooking Time: 6 minutes
Servings: 4

Ingredients:

- ½ cup water
- ¼ cup granulated sugar
- 2 large fresh dill sprigs, stemmed
- 2 large fresh basil sprigs, stemmed
- 1 cup ice water
- 2 tablespoons fresh lemon juice

Preparation:

1. In a small saucepan, add sugar and water and over medium heat and cook for about five minutes or until the sugar is dissolved, stirring continuously.
2. Stir in the herb sprigs and remove from the heat.
3. Add the ice water and lemon juice and stir to combine.
4. Transfer the mixture into an empty Ninja CREAMi pint container.
5. Cover the container with storage lid and freeze for 24 hours.
6. After 24 hours, remove the lid from container and arrange into the Outer Bowl of Ninja CREAMi.
7. Install the Creamerizer Paddle onto the lid of Outer Bowl.
8. Then rotate the lid clockwise to lock.
9. Press Power button to turn on the unit.
10. Then press Sorbet button.
11. When the program is completed, turn the Outer Bowl and release it from the machine.
12. Transfer the sorbet into serving bowls and serve immediately.

Serving Suggestions: Serve with the garnishing of fresh herbs.

Variation Tip: Use herbs of your choice.

Nutritional Information per Serving:
Calories: 51 | Fat: 0.1g|Sat Fat: 0g.1|Carbohydrates: 13.1g|Fiber: 0.1g|Sugar: 12.7g|Protein: 0.2g

Peach Sorbet

Preparation Time: 10 minutes
Servings: 4

Ingredients:

- 1 cup passionfruit seltzer
- 3 tablespoons agave nectar
- 1 (15¼-ounce) can peaches in heavy syrup, drained

Preparation:

1. In a bowl, add the seltzer and agave and beat until agave is dissolved.
2. Place the peaches into an empty Ninja CREAMi pint container and top with seltzer mixture.
3. Cover the container with storage lid and freeze for 24 hours.
4. After 24 hours, remove the lid from container and arrange into the Outer Bowl of Ninja CREAMi.
5. Install the Creamerizer Paddle onto the lid of Outer Bowl.
6. Then rotate the lid clockwise to lock.
7. Press Power button to turn on the unit.
8. Then press Sorbet button.
9. When the program is completed, turn the Outer Bowl and release it from the machine.
10. Transfer the sorbet into serving bowls and serve immediately.

Serving Suggestions: Serve with the garnishing of fresh mint leaves.

Variation Tip: Agave nectar can be replaced with maple syrup.

Nutritional Information per Serving:
Calories: 271 | Fat: 1.5g|Sat Fat: 0g|Carbohydrates: 65.4g|Fiber: 9.5g|Sugar: 64.6g|Protein: 5.3g

Plum Sorbet

Preparation Time: 10 minutes
Servings: 4

Ingredients:

- 1 (20-ounce) can plums

Preparation:

1. Place the plums into an empty Ninja CREAMi pint container.
2. Cover the container with storage lid and freeze for 24 hours.
3. After 24 hours, remove the lid from container and arrange into the Outer Bowl of Ninja CREAMi.
4. Install the Creamerizer Paddle onto the lid of Outer Bowl.
5. Then rotate the lid clockwise to lock.
6. Press Power button to turn on the unit.
7. Then press Sorbet button.
8. When the program is completed, turn the Outer Bowl and release it from the machine.
9. Transfer the sorbet into serving bowls and serve immediately.

Serving Suggestions: Serve with the garnishing of coconut flakes.

Variation Tip: You can use peaches sin this recipe too.

Nutritional Information per Serving:
Calories: 150 | Fat: 1g|Sat Fat: 0g|Carbohydrates: 40g|Fiber: 4.5g|Sugar: 35g|Protein: 2.5g

Raspberry Sorbet

Preparation Time: 10 minutes
Servings: 4

Ingredients:

- 3 cups fresh raspberries
- ⅓ cup water
- ⅓ cup sugar
- ¾ cup berry punch

Preparation:

1. In a high-speed blender, add all the ingredients and pulse until smooth.
2. Transfer the mixture into an empty Ninja CREAMi pint container.
3. Cover the container with storage lid and freeze for 24 hours.
4. After 24 hours, remove the lid from container and arrange into the Outer Bowl of Ninja CREAMi.
5. Install the Creamerizer Paddle onto the lid of Outer Bowl.
6. Then rotate the lid clockwise to lock.
7. Press Power button to turn on the unit.
8. Then press Sorbet button.
9. When the program is completed, turn the Outer Bowl and release it from the machine.
10. Transfer the sorbet into serving bowls and serve immediately.

Serving Suggestions: Serve with the drizzling of chocolate syrup.

Variation Tip: You can use citrus berry punch too.

Nutritional Information per Serving:
Calories: 135 | Fat: 0.6g|Sat Fat: 0g|Carbohydrates: 33.7g|Fiber: 6g|Sugar: 26.4g|Protein: 1.1g

Strawberry Sorbet

Preparation Time: 10 minutes
Servings: 4

Ingredients:

- 6 ounces daiquiri mix
- 2 ounces rum
- ½ cup frozen strawberries
- ½ cup simple syrup

Preparation:

1. In an empty Ninja CREAMi pint container, add all the ingredients and mix well.
2. Cover the container with storage lid and freeze for 24 hours.
3. After 24 hours, remove the lid from container and arrange into the Outer Bowl of Ninja CREAMi.
4. Install the Creamerizer Paddle onto the lid of Outer Bowl.
5. Then rotate the lid clockwise to lock.
6. Press Power button to turn on the unit.
7. Then press Sorbet button.
8. When the program is completed, turn the Outer Bowl and release it from the machine.
9. Transfer the sorbet into serving bowls and serve immediately.

Serving Suggestions: Serve with the garnishing of fresh strawberry slices.

Variation Tip: Don't thaw the strawberries.

Nutritional Information per Serving:
Calories: 330 | Fat: 0.1g|Sat Fat: 0g|Carbohydrates: 72.6g|Fiber: 0.4g|Sugar: 37.7g|Protein: 0.1g

Mixed Berries Sorbet

Preparation Time: 10 minutes
Servings: 4

Ingredients:

- 1 cup blueberries
- 1 cup raspberries
- 1 cup strawberries, hulled and quartered

Preparation:

1. In an empty Ninja CREAMi pint container, place the berries and with a potato masher, mash until well combined.
2. Cover the container with storage lid and freeze for 24 hours.
3. After 24 hours, remove the lid from container and arrange into the outer bowl of Ninja CREAMi.
4. Install the Creamerizer Paddle onto the lid of Outer Bowl.
5. Then rotate the lid clockwise to lock.
6. Press Power button to turn on the unit.
7. Then press Sorbet button.
8. When the program is completed, turn the Outer Bowl and release it from the machine.
9. Transfer the sorbet into serving bowls and serve immediately.

Serving Suggestions: Serve with the garnishing of chocolate chips.

Variation Tip: You can use berries of your choice.

Nutritional Information per Serving:
Calories: 48 | Fat: .40g|Sat Fat: 0g|Carbohydrates: 11.7g| Fiber: 3.6g|Sugar: 6.7g|Protein: 0.9g

Grape Sorbet

Preparation Time: 10 minutes
Servings: 4

Ingredients:

- ¾ cup frozen grape juice concentrate
- 1½ cups water
- 1 tablespoon fresh lemon juice

Preparation:

1. In a bowl, add all the ingredients and beat until well combined.
2. Transfer the mixture into an empty Ninja CREAMi pint container.
3. Cover the container with storage lid and freeze for 24 hours.
4. After 24 hours, remove the lid from container and arrange into the Outer Bowl of Ninja CREAMi.
5. Install the Creamerizer Paddle onto the lid of Outer Bowl.
6. Then rotate the lid clockwise to lock.
7. Press Power button to turn on the unit.
8. Then press Sorbet button.
9. When the program is completed, turn the Outer Bowl and release it from the machine.
10. Transfer the sorbet into serving bowls and serve immediately.

Serving Suggestions: Serve with the topping of chopped nuts.

Variation Tip: Use freshly squeezed lemon juice.

Nutritional Information per Serving:
Calories: 25 | Fat: 0.1g|Sat Fat: 0g|Carbohydrates: 6.1g| Fiber: 0.1g|Sugar: 6g|Protein: 0.1g

Kiwi & Strawberry Sorbet

Preparation Time: 10 minutes
Servings: 4

Ingredients:

- 2 cups frozen sliced strawberries
- 4 kiwis, peeled and cut into 1-inch pieces
- ¼ cup agave nectar
- ¼ cup water

Preparation:

1. In a high-speed blender, add all the ingredients and pulse until smooth.
2. Transfer the mixture into an empty Ninja CREAMi pint container.
3. Cover the container with storage lid and freeze for 24 hours.
4. After 24 hours, remove the lid from container and arrange into the Outer Bowl of Ninja CREAMi.
5. Install the Creamerizer Paddle onto the lid of Outer Bowl.
6. Then rotate the lid clockwise to lock.
7. Press Power button to turn on the unit.
8. Then press Sorbet button.
9. When the program is completed, turn the Outer Bowl and release it from the machine.
10. Transfer the sorbet into serving bowls and serve immediately.

Serving Suggestions: Serve with the garnishing of shredded coconut.

Variation Tip: You can berries of your choice.

Nutritional Information per Serving:
Calories: 131 | Fat: 0.4g|Sat Fat: 0g|Carbohydrates: 33.7g| Fiber: 4.8g|Sugar: 26.3g|Protein: 0.9g

Pomegranate & Blueberry Sorbet

Preparation Time: 10 minutes
Servings: 4

Ingredients:

- 1 (15-ounce) can blueberries in light syrup
- ½ cup pomegranate juice

Preparation:

1. In an empty Ninja CREAMi pint container, place the blueberries and top with syrup
2. Add in the pomegranate juice and stir to combine.
3. Cover the container with storage lid and freeze for 24 hours.
4. After 24 hours, remove the lid from container and arrange into the Outer bowl of Ninja CREAMi.
5. Install the Creamerizer Paddle onto the lid of Outer Bowl.
6. Then rotate the lid clockwise to lock.
7. Press Power button to turn on the unit.
8. Then press Sorbet button.
9. When the program is completed, turn the Outer Bowl and release it from the machine.
10. Transfer the sorbet into serving bowls and serve immediately.

Serving Suggestions: Serve with garnishing of fresh blueberries.

Variation Tip: Use sweetened pomegranate juice.

Nutritional Information per Serving:
Calories: 101 | Fat: 0.4g|Sat Fat: 0g|Carbohydrates: 25.2g| Fiber: 2.6g|Sugar: 19g|Protein: 0.8g

Pineapple & Rum Sorbet

Preparation Time: 10 minutes
Servings: 4

Ingredients:

- ¾ cup piña colada mix
- ¼ cup rum
- 2 tablespoons granulated sugar
- 1½ cups frozen pineapple chunks

Preparation:

1. In a high-speed blender, add all the ingredients and pulse until smooth.
2. Transfer the mixture into an empty Ninja CREAMi pint container.
3. Cover the container with storage lid and freeze for 24 hours.
4. After 24 hours, remove the lid from container and arrange into the Outer Bowl of Ninja CREAMi.
5. Install the Creamerizer Paddle onto the lid of Outer Bowl.
6. Then rotate the lid clockwise to lock.
7. Press Power button to turn on the unit.
8. Then press Sorbet button.
9. When the program is completed, turn the Outer Bowl and release it from the machine.
10. Transfer the sorbet into serving bowls and serve immediately.

Serving Suggestions: Serve with the garnishing of fresh mint leaves.

Variation Tip: use white rum.

Nutritional Information per Serving:
Calories: 102 | Fat: 0.2g|Sat Fat: 0g|Carbohydrates: 17.6g| Fiber: 1.8g|Sugar: 14.4g|Protein: 0.6g

Mango Sorbet

Preparation Time: 15 minutes
Servings: 4

Ingredients:

- 4 cups mangoes, peeled, pitted and chopped
- ½ cup water
- ⅓-½ cup sugar
- ¼ cup fresh lime juice
- 2 tablespoons Chamoy

Preparation:

1. In a high-speed blender, add mangoes and water and pulse until smooth.
2. Through a fine-mesh strainer, strain the mango puree into a large bowl.
3. Add the sugar, lime juice and chamoy and stir to combine.
4. Transfer the mixture into an empty Ninja CREAMi pint container.
5. Cover the container with storage lid and freeze for 24 hours.
6. After 24 hours, remove the lid from container and arrange into the Outer Bowl of Ninja CREAMi.
7. Install the Creamerizer Paddle onto the lid of Outer Bowl.
8. Then rotate the lid clockwise to lock.
9. Press Power button to turn on the unit.
10. Then press Sorbet button.
11. When the program is completed, turn the Outer Bowl and release it from the machine.
12. Transfer the sorbet into serving bowls and serve immediately.

Serving Suggestions: Serve with the topping of coconut.

Variation Tip: make sure to use ripe mango.

Nutritional Information per Serving:
Calories: 168 | Fat: 5.6g|Sat Fat: 0.2g|Carbohydrates: 42g| Fiber: 2.6g|Sugar: 39.2g|Protein: 1.4g

Acai & Fruit Sorbet

Preparation Time: 10 minutes
Servings: 4

Ingredients:

- 1 packet frozen acai
- ½ cup blackberries
- ½ cup banana, peeled and sliced
- ¼ cup granulated sugar
- 1 cup water

Preparation:

1. In a high-speed blender, add all the ingredients and pulse until smooth.
2. Transfer the mixture into an empty Ninja CREAMi pint container.
3. Cover the container with storage lid and freeze for 24 hours.
4. After 24 hours, remove the lid from container and arrange into the Outer Bowl of Ninja CREAMi.
5. Install the Creamerizer Paddle onto the lid of Outer Bowl.
6. Then rotate the lid clockwise to lock.
7. Press Power button to turn on the unit.
8. Then press Sorbet button.
9. When the program is completed, turn the Outer Bowl and release it from the machine.
10. Transfer the sorbet into serving bowls and serve immediately.

Serving Suggestions: Serve with the garnishing of fresh berries.

Variation Tip: You can use berries of your choice in this recipe.

Nutritional Information per Serving:
Calories: 86 | Fat: 0.2g|Sat Fat: 0g|Carbohydrates: 22.3g|Fiber: 1.7g|Sugar: 19.2g|Protein: 0.5g

Conclusion

The Ninja CREAMi is one of the most efficient ice cream makers which can prepare milkshakes, sorbets, smoothies and ice creams in considerably less time. The device offers preset functions for every recipe and the control panel is extremely user friendly. The device can be easily cleaned by putting the lid, paddle and containers can be cleaned in a dishwasher. However, never put the motor base in any liquid; rather, use a damp cloth to clean it efficiently. The Ninja CREAMi is a blessing and lifesaver for ice cream lovers as you can make homemade and nutritious ice cream in very little time and effort.

Appendix Measurement Conversion Chart

WEIGHT EQUIVALENTS

US STANDARD	METRIC (APPROXIMATE)
1 ounce	28 g
2 ounces	57 g
5 ounces	142 g
10 ounces	284 g
15 ounces	425 g
16 ounces (1 pound)	455 g
1.5 pounds	680 g
2 pounds	907 g

VOLUME EQUIVALENTS (LIQUID)

US STANDARD	US STANDARD (OUNCES)	METRIC (APPROXIMATE)
2 tablespoons	1 fl.oz	30 mL
¼ cup	2 fl.oz	60 mL
½ cup	4 fl.oz	120 mL
1 cup	8 fl.oz	240 mL
1½ cup	12 fl.oz	355 mL
2 cups or 1 pint	16 fl.oz	475 mL
4 cups or 1 quart	32 fl.oz	1 L
1 gallon	128 fl.oz	4 L

TEMPERATURES EQUIVALENTS

FAHRENHEIT(F)	CELSIUS(C) (APPROXIMATE)
225 °F	107 °C
250 °F	120 °C
275 °F	135 °C
300 °F	150 °C
325 °F	160 °C
350 °F	180 °C
375 °F	190 °C
400 °F	205 °C
425 °F	220 °C
450 °F	235 °C
475 °F	245 °C
500 °F	260 °C

VOLUME EQUIVALENTS (DRY)

US STANDARD	METRIC (APPROXIMATE)
⅛ teaspoon	0.5 mL
¼ teaspoon	1 mL
½ teaspoon	2 mL
¾ teaspoon	4 mL
1 teaspoon	5 mL
1 tablespoon	15 mL
¼ cup	59 mL
½ cup	118 mL
¾ cup	177 mL
1 cup	235 mL
2 cups	475 mL
3 cups	700 mL
4 cups	1 L

Made in the USA
Thornton, CO
10/17/23 10:22:58

251ec07c-2132-4344-b067-30a5f5cede5aR01